Accelerated Reader
Level 3.7

Review
Gr3-5 --- Nine-year-old Patrick Doyle promises his buddies that his
baseball hero, New York Giant, Larry Doyle, will come play with them
against the Copperheads, a rough gang. Doyle does show up but
coaches Patrick instead, and the Copperheads are beaten and chased off
the field. Set in 1915, this short work of fiction portrays the
Irish-American lifestyle in New York City and the importance of
baseball to the youth of America, regardless of ethnicity. The book also
contains a short history and glossary in the back to aid in understanding
the time period and Irish character of Patrick. Armstrong's rich and
lyrical text is peppered with black and white illustrations, which together
portray the hilarious antics of Patrick and his Irish friends. Along with
recommending this book for a library collection, it would also make a
great read-aloud in the classroom. Angela Hansen, Wayne State
College, Wayne, NE.

Patrick Doyle is Full of Blarney

Other Books by Jennifer Armstrong

Steal Away
Hugh Can Do
Chin Yu Min and the Ginger Cat
Little Salt Lick and the Sun King
King Crow
Black-Eyed Susan

Patrick Doyle is Full of Blarney

by Jennifer Armstrong

illustrated by
Krista Brauckmann-Towns

A STEPPING STONE BOOK

Random House 🏠 New York

Library of Congress Cataloging-in-Publication Data
Armstrong, Jennifer, 1961–
Patrick Doyle is full of blarney / by Jennifer Armstrong; illustrated by Krista
Brauckmann-Towns. p. cm. A stepping stone book.
SUMMARY: Nine-year-old Patrick promises his buddies that his baseball hero will
come to their playground in Hell's Kitchen, bat for him, and chase the
Copperheads out.
ISBN 0-679-87285-X (trade) — ISBN 0-679-97285-4 (lib. bdg.)
1. Irish Americans—Juvenile fiction. [1. Irish Americans—Fiction. 2. Baseball—
Fiction.] I. Brauckmann-Towns. Krista, ill. II. Title.
PZ7.A73367Pat 1996 [Fic]—dc20 95-24754

For Jimmy, from Shillyshally Gilgargle

Contents

1

I Introduce Myself

What with it being the first day of summer, it was pretty hot. So I went up on the roof.

Sure enough, there was a breeze blowing in off the Hudson River. I watched the breeze flap the laundry on the clotheslines. All those shirts and dresses were waving their arms up and down, up and down. It looked like a crowd of fans cheering a home run in a big ballpark.

I took my hat off and did a bow. Then I squared off over a make-believe home plate and squinted across the roof.

"*Crack!* A line drive to the end of the earth! Slugger Doyle does it again!"

I made a roaring noise into my hands. It sounds like a big crowd going wild if you do it right.

Then I took a slow jog around the bases. First to the first chimney, then to Mickey O'Malley's pigeon coop, then to the other chimney. Then it was back to home plate. The tar on the roof was soft and warm under my shoes.

"Hey, Patrick!"

My pal Joey Flynn jumped onto our roof from his roof next door.

It's not much of a jump. It's more like a big step, since all the tenements are so close together. If you live higher than the sixth floor, it's faster to travel by roof than go down all the stairs to the avenue. Besides, if you go by roof, you get a fly-ball's view of all Manhattan.

"Whatcha doing?" Joey asked.

"Nothing."

We looked at the river. Ferries chugged back and forth from Manhattan to New Jersey. There were plenty of tugboats and barges and oyster boats.

But there weren't many ocean liners at the piers. A war was going on in Europe, and the Germans had sunk a ritzy passenger ship out in the Atlantic Ocean somewhere. That was back in May. Since then, most people were too scared to travel. I bet you probably couldn't fill a streetcar with the folks who were willing to get on an ocean liner.

And by June, grownups in the neighborhood were yakking about the United States getting into that war.

But grownups scare easy. Didn't they realize nothing could happen until after the World Series?

"Come on, let's climb up the pigeon coop," I said, and waved my arm.

The pigeons went *woo-woo*, *woo-woo* and

skedaddled away from us. We shaded our eyes from the sun and looked north.

"I wish we could see the Polo Grounds," I said. "I'd give anything to watch the Giants play any old time we wanted."

Joey sighed. "It's not fair we live so far downtown."

We were much too far away to see the ballpark. It was way uptown, at 155th Street. And where were we? Way down in Hell's Kitchen, on 38th Street on the West Side of New York City.

But I could picture the ballpark in my head like it was on the next block.

Sometimes the gang and I rode the electric trolley up there to take in a game. We always sat on the cliff overlooking the ballpark. The cliff was called Coogan's Bluff, and it was really the best spot to watch from. Besides, it was free.

Of course, you couldn't exactly see the

faces of the players from up on the bluff. But we didn't need to. We knew who played every position. And naturally, we knew each player's batting stance.

I always kept my eye on second base when the Giants had the field. Second base was the property of Laughing Larry Doyle, captain of the team. He was my favorite player, what with my last name being Doyle too and seeing as how second base was my position. Doyle was also a league leader in hits.

Take him all together, I always said, Larry Doyle was an all-around swell player. I've been copying his batting style, since it's sure working for him. I even bat left and throw right, just like Larry.

"Guess what," I said to Joey. "I wrote a fan letter to Larry Doyle."

His eyes went as round as a pair of hanging curveballs. "Quit pulling my leg!"

"I wrote him a letter and sent it to the

Polo Grounds. I guess I got as much right as anyone else to write him a letter," I said. "And besides, I bet he writes back."

Joey laughed. "Sure, Pat. And someday an Irishman will grow potatoes on the moon."

2

The History of Baseball According to Me

I stopped to pick up my bat. It was nothing more than an old broomstick wrapped 'round and 'round with string at one end to make it thicker. Then off we went to our own ballpark.

The grassy paddock behind Gilhooley's Brewery on 35th was where we played ball. The brewery had begun using motor trucks for delivery, so it didn't need its draft horses any longer. There was only one horse left, a giant old mare with a gray velvet muzzle. Miss Barley was her name, and she was glad to share her paddock with us.

Sometimes you'd see the Irish brewers

emptying the last drops from beer barrels onto the grass in that paddock. Perhaps beer makes a good fertilizer, I'm not sure. I do know that it was the greenest grass I'd ever seen. And Miss Barley kept it cropped short and as velvety as her own nose. So take it all together, it was one swell ball field.

Joey and I ducked through the gap in the fence. Seamus O'Roarke, Billy Pogue, Nat Cooley, and most of our other pals were already there. They were playing pepper and flies-up, with Billy whacking fly balls.

Joey and I watched Nat try to field the ball.

"I got it, I got it!" he called, running backwards and backwards and backwards.

He bumped into Miss Barley and fell onto a pile of horse manure. The ball sailed past, bounced off the tall brick wall of the brewery, and fell to the ground. Miss Barley kept munching grass. There was green spit in the corners of her mouth.

"Ready for the big leagues, Billy Pogue?" I called.

"Hey, Patrick! Hi, Joey!" The guys waved, and Nat picked up the ball and threw it to me.

It was a stinger, but I caught it.

Joey was looking around at our friends. A funny look came over him.

"I just noticed something," he said, scratching his head.

"What's that?" Seamus asked.

"All us fellows here that play ball are Irish," Joey said.

I tossed the ball from one hand to the other. "That's only natural, as baseball is a naturally Irish sport."

"Isn't!" Nat said. "It was invented right here in America, anyone knows that." He twirled one finger beside his ear to show I was loony.

It didn't bother me a bit. "I'm not saying it wasn't invented here. I'm saying that it's a naturally Irish sport and I'll tell you why."

"Here comes a line of blarney," Billy said. "Pat's such a talker."

But the fellows gathered around.

"Aren't the very finest players in the game Irish?" I asked. "I give you Ed Delahanty and his brothers. There's Nixey Callahan and

Charley O'Leary and Deacon McGuire."

"Don't forget Roger Bresnahan, the Duke of Tralee," Seamus added.

"And Stuffy McInnis and Brickyard Kennedy and Wickey McAvoy, and let's not leave out Ty Cobb," I went on.

"Ty Cobb's as American as President Wilson!" Joey shouted. "He's the Georgia Peach."

"But Cobb's an Irish name," I said. "If you look high enough in his family tree, you'll find potatoes growing on it."

"And my ma can cook them," Joey said with a laugh.

"Now to continue," I said. "What else is a shillelagh but a baseball bat? And what do the three leaves of the shamrock mean? Three strikes you're out and three outs to an inning, that's what."

I bent down and plucked a three-leafed clover from the field and held it up. The boys nodded. They could see I had a point.

"The manager of the Giants is John McGraw. And to top it all off, the National League was founded on St. Patrick's Day," I finished. "And if that doesn't make baseball a naturally Irish sport, then I don't know what does."

Nobody said a word. I kept tossing the ball from one hand to the other. Take it all together, it was a pretty good explanation. I thought I might even write it in another letter to Laughing Larry Doyle, my hero.

We stood there on the green, green grass in the sunshine, thinking of how lucky we were to be Irish.

That's when the Copperheads showed up.

3

I Offer a Challenge

The Copperheads were a rough gang.

Many of them had no mothers or fathers. They lived here, there, and everywhere around Hell's Kitchen. Some of them were newsboys, and earned nickels and dimes selling papers. But mostly they just roamed around and made trouble. They picked pockets, stole from pushcarts, that sort of thing. None of them were Irish. Take them all together, they were as welcome as whooping cough. Until that day in June, they had never found our green piece of Ireland behind Gilhooley's.

"Hey, look here," the leader said.

He was a big fellow with a broken nose—
a fighter, even though he probably was the
same age as us. That is, nine. We all knew his
name was Pug.

Pug bashed the loose board out of the
fence to make the entrance bigger. He and his
pals crawled in through the hole.

None of us Irish kids said anything. We
just watched those Copperheads slink around
with their hands in their pockets, looking the
place over. Joey looked at me and gulped.

"Beat it," Pug said to us. He jerked one
thumb over his shoulder.

"But this is our field," Nat spoke up. "We
were here first."

Pug walked over to Nat, who was a short
kid. Without warning, he punched Nat in the
stomach. Nat fell to his knees and made a
squeaking sound.

"And now *we're* here. Beat it," Pug said
again.

Three of his buddies lined up behind him

and stared at us. They were all very big, and very tough. They didn't look like they played fair.

Now, many people say that the Irish like to fight. But our gang of Irish ballplayers was not up to fighting the Copperheads.

But that didn't mean we would just give up.

"Why don't you play with us?" I suggested. "Let's have a game. We've had enough infield practice."

Pug looked at his pals and laughed. "He's so funny he could be in vaudeville. What a comedy act!"

The other Copperheads snickered.

Then Pug stepped up to me and looked me right in the eyes. "I'll *play* with you. I'll use you as the bat and your runty friend as the ball. Now scram."

Joey, Seamus, and the others turned and were about to walk away. But I didn't move.

"Wait!" I said. "We challenge you!"

"Patrick!" Joey looked scared. "Shut up!"

I kept my eyes on Pug. When I get angry or nervous, I talk. So that's what I did. I talked.

"We challenge you to a game. The winner gets the field, and the losers never come back," I said quickly. "Anytime you say the word."

Pug narrowed his eyes. "You're Patrick Doyle, right? I seen you around."

I felt like I had a knuckleball stuck in my throat. "Yes."

"Now listen to me, Patrick Doyle. Copperheads don't take such *easy* challenges. It ain't good for our reputation."

"Then we'll make it more interesting," I went on. I could see Joey trying to wave me away. He wanted me to shut up and go, but I wouldn't move. "Doyle will hit a home run for us—over the fence," I added, pointing to the fence on the far side of the paddock.

Pug snorted through his nose. "You?

Patrick Doyle is going to hit one over the fence?"

I stood my ground. "*Doyle* will hit one over the fence," I said carefully. "If so, you leave. If not, you can beat us all up."

The Copperheads began to laugh and slap their knees. Pug looked me up and down. A cocky smile spread across his broke-nosed face. "We can beat you up anyway. But you're on. You can even choose the time."

"Fourth of July," I said. "Independence Day. That's two weeks from now, and it'll give us all a chance to practice up."

"Practice all you want, Doyle," Pug said. "It ain't gonna help."

"Just keep your word," I said. "We'll keep ours."

Pug and his gang slapped each other on the back. They laughed as they left the field. Anyone could see they figured they had already won.

But I knew something they didn't. The

hitter who put one over the fence on the Fourth of July wasn't going to be *Patrick* Doyle. It was going to be *Larry* Doyle, slugging champ of the New York Giants.

I just had to get him to play for us.

4

A Plan

As soon as the Copperheads had oozed out through the fence, Joey and Seamus and the other fellows let out a groan all together.

"Are you crazy?" Billy cried. "You've never hit the ball over the fence, Patrick Doyle!"

"What have you gotten us into?" Joey clapped both hands over his eyes and shook his head.

I flashed my friends a carefree smile. "Relax. I don't have to hit a home run over the fence."

Nat sighed. "So we get beat up and lose our field. I get it. You're trying to kill us."

I couldn't help laughing. "You should see your faces! I got the whole thing figured out. *Larry* Doyle is going to hit the ball over the fence, you crybabies. Laughing Larry Doyle! Not me."

I didn't exactly think they would cheer. But I did expect them to look a little happier.

Seamus hung his bat over his shoulder and began to leave. One by one, the rest of the fellows followed him. In no time, Joey and I were alone on the field with Miss Barley.

"They don't think I can get him to come," I said. I rubbed Miss Barley's nose. She smelled sweet, like grass. "I'll write him another letter and explain the whole thing."

Joey picked at a scab on his elbow. "Doyle didn't answer your first letter, did he?" Joey asked quietly.

"No. Not exactly. Not at all. Come on."

I led the way across the field and through the fence. Joey tagged after me, like he always does. We went down the alley, past Poole's glue factory, and out onto Tenth Avenue.

There was a doozie of a traffic jam, as usual. Automobiles and motor trucks and trolleys and horse-drawn wagons were all crammed together in the street. You could hear people yelling at each other in about six different languages—English, Yiddish, Italian, and a few I didn't recognize.

Joey and I dodged pushcarts and sweet-potato vendors and headed for our favorite nickelodeon. It was cool and dim inside. The air was filled with the high stink of tobacco juice from the spittoons.

A fat kid with broken shoes was using my personal favorite nickel machine. That was the one that played a movie of Honus Wagner batting, fielding, and pitching at Forbes Field. Take him all together, Honus Wagner was the best player ever. No offense to my hero, Larry Doyle.

"Patrick?" Joey asked. "What if Doyle doesn't come?"

"He will." I stared at the back of the fat kid's head. I wanted the kid to leave so I could watch the Honus Wagner movie myself. I raised my voice a little. "Wasn't that Charlie Chaplin signing autographs outside?"

"Where?" Joey asked, looking confused.

The fat kid turned to look at me. He looked at the door, and back to the Honus Wagner movie. Then he ran to the door. I stepped up to the machine and got to watch the end of the movie on the kid's nickel.

"This is what I'll write in my letter," I told Joey, keeping my eyes on the screen. "I've got it written in my head already:

"Dear Mr. Laughing Larry Doyle,

"You'll really laugh when you hear this one. I played a trick on some tough kids called the Copperheads. I said Doyle would hit a homer over the fence. They thought I meant me, Patrick Doyle. But I meant you. If you don't go to bat for us on the Fourth of July, we'll lose our field. It's the best place to play ball in all of New York City, except for the Polo Grounds. We're behind Gilhooley's Brewery on 35th.

"Your fan, Patrick Doyle."

"Think he'll come?" Joey asked.

"I'm sure of it," I said, just as the movie screen went black.

5

I Write a Letter

That was exactly, word for word, what I wrote in my letter when I got home. My penmanship was not very good, though. I had to write the letter seven times before I had a copy without too many ink blots or smears.

I wrote at the kitchen table while my Granny McGaffigan sat by the window. She was mending. She chatted across the air shaft with Mrs. Rosenkranz, who was doing mending by *her* window. Mrs. Rosenkranz lived in Joey's building on the same floor as us.

"Warm day, isn't it, Mrs. Rosenkranz?" Granny said, sewing a button.

Mrs. Rosenkranz nodded, and all her

chins nodded, too. "Such warmth!"

"What I wouldn't give to be back in Ireland!" Granny exclaimed. "I worry the heavenly saints are angry so many of us left home. *That's* why we must live in Hell's Kitchen, as a punishment."

"No, no, Mrs. McGaffigan. You are lucky to be in America. This is the golden land," Mrs. Rosenkranz said. She wiped her forehead with a hanky.

Granny put her mending down in her lap. "And Ireland is the green land. Oh, that blessed isle! Blessed by Saint Patrick, who drove off the snakes."

"How did he do that, Mrs. McGaffigan?" Mrs. Rosenkranz asked.

"Well, now, it's a funny thing you should ask," my granny began. "For it was truly a miracle. First he took a stick and a drum. Then he beat the drum and beat the drum, and the snakes fled before him into the sea. Tap-tappity-tap—and off they went!"

"Just like that?"

Granny McGaffigan nodded wisely. "Indeed. But then he beat so hard that he put a hole in the drum with his stick. And what should happen then?"

Mrs. Rosenkranz looked astonished. "I don't know!"

"An angel came down and mended it for him on the spot," my granny said with a proud smile. "And St. Patrick was able to chase away the snakes for good. There's a poem, to be sure:

"Success to bold St. Patrick's fist.
He was a saint so clever.
He gave the sneaking snakes a twist
And banished them forever!"

Mrs. Rosenkranz leaned out the window to look into our kitchen. "And this is who you are named for, Patrick?"

I folded my letter neatly and put it in an envelope. "That's right."

"And are you as clever as St. Patrick?" Mrs. Rosenkranz asked.

"I think so, Mrs. Rosenkranz. I sure hope so."

I smiled at our neighbor. Then I wrote

Larry Doyle
Captain of the Giants
Polo Grounds

on the envelope. Now I just had to wait.

6

Joey and I Meet a Giant

I waited three days, and I still didn't get an answer to my *first* letter.

I didn't let it worry me, though. The gang and I practiced every day on our ball field. Every time someone asked if Larry Doyle was coming, I said sure. Joey was the only one who knew I hadn't gotten a letter yet.

Joey and I played pepper on the roof of our building after breakfast each morning. We also sat talking for a while on the pigeon coop each day. Mostly we talked about which baseball players we would like to be. We didn't mention that our game with the Copperheads was only a week away.

31

I was also working on a new ball in honor of our great game. I had bought a solid rubber ball from the five-and-dime. It was about the size of a chestnut. Now I was wrapping it 'round and 'round with string to build it up.

"Granny McGaffigan promised to sew a cover on it," I said.

Joey squeezed it and tossed it from hand to hand. "It's a good one."

"But I wish I had a better bat," I said. I frowned at my old broomstick leaning against the coop. It almost made me ashamed to invite Larry to our game.

"I've got an idea," I said, jumping back down to the roof.

Joey jumped down after me. "What?"

"We're going to go see Larry Doyle. The Giants are playing Boston tomorrow. If we hurry, we can catch them before they get on the train this morning. I've got another letter all written, and we can hand it to him."

In a flash, we ran down all the stairs to

the street. Then we were on our way to the biggest train station in the world. Grand Central Terminal, that is.

It was four blocks uptown and seven blocks east. By the time we skedaddled up there I felt like I had run the bases sixteen times. Panting, Joey and I stood at the top of the stairs looking down into the Grand Concourse.

When they called it *Grand*, they weren't kidding. Enormous windows towered on each side. The roof soared way above the giant room. And when I tipped my head back to look up, I saw there were stars painted on the blue ceiling. Some of the stars even had electric lights shining in them.

The Concourse was crawling with people and noisier than a ballpark during a pennant game. Travelers in summer straw hats stood at the gates with their tickets. Porters in red caps pushed luggage around on carts. Newsboys shouted "Getcher paper!" Take it all together, it was a swell train station.

"Hey, mister," I said, tugging on a man's arm.

He took his cigar from his mouth. "What is it, sonny?"

"Where's the train the Giants take?"

"Heck, how should I know? But there's someone who might," he said. He pointed down the steps with his cigar.

We looked, and we nearly fainted dead away. The one and only, the great, the magnificent Christy Mathewson was standing at the bottom of the staircase signing autographs for a crowd of fans.

Joey looked like a statue.

Mathewson lifted his straw hat to his fans and headed across the Concourse.

"Come on!" I grabbed Joey's arm and pulled him down the slippery marble steps.

At the same time, I dragged my letter out of my pocket. I knew we didn't have much time.

"There he goes!" Joey said, hanging on to his hat.

We zigzagged through the crowd. A fat lady said "Whoops!" as I whisked past her.

Beside Gate 21 was a signboard that said SPECIAL. Just before Mathewson disappeared through the gate, we galloped up behind him.

"Wait!" I shouted. I waved my letter for Larry Doyle in the air.

The Giants' star pitcher turned around with a smile. Before I could catch my breath to speak, Mathewson took the letter from my hand. He took out his pen and autographed the back of the envelope. Then he handed it

back to me and went through the gate.

"But—!" I panted. I started to follow him down the ramp.

The conductor stepped in front of me. "Sorry, kid. Players only."

He clanged the gate in our faces.

A shutout.

7

Tap-Tappity-Tap

"Now what?" Joey asked as we plodded back to Tenth Avenue.

"I'm thinking."

"Try thinking a little faster," my pal suggested. "Here comes Pug."

We stopped on the sidewalk outside a saloon. The El rumbled by on its overhead tracks as Pug came swaggering toward us. He had a know-it-all smile on his face. He stopped and looked us up and down real slow. Then he spit on the ground.

"Help me here," he began in a fake-friendly voice. "I can't make up my mind where to punch you first after our game."

Joey squeezed his hat in his hands and looked wide-eyed at me. But I still figured the saints were on my side.

"I didn't know you *had* a mind to make up," I said in the same fake-friendly voice.

Pug looked surprised, and then he looked mean. "I made it up just now. I'm going to punch you in your big fat mouth."

"How are you going to do that when you're kicked out of our ball field?"

"Patriiiiiick!" Joey's voice went up in a squeak.

"You stupid Irish potato-eater," Pug snarled. "Maybe you oughta go up to St. Patrick's Cathedral and say your prayers. I'm going to make mashed potatoes out of you."

He shouldered and shoved between us and strode away.

Joey was shaking his head from side to side. He looked just like a catcher who can't stop signaling.

"Give me a nickel," I said.

"We're gonna die."

"Just give me a nickel," I said again. I held out my hand.

"What do you want it for?" Joey asked. "I only got one."

"We're running out of time. I'm going to send a telegram." I started for the Western Union office on the corner.

Joey ran to keep up.

"Who to?" he wanted to know.

We went inside.

"Who else?" I whispered. Clerks in arm garters and green eyeshades were tapping away at the telegraph machines. I took a form off the counter and found a pencil stub on the floor.

MOST URGENT YOU BAT FOR US
ON JULY FOURTH STOP WE'RE
MASHED POTATOES IF YOU
DON'T COME STOP HELP ME
DRIVE THOSE SNAKES AWAY
STOP SIGNED PAT DOYLE STOP

"Larry Doyle, at Visitors' Clubhouse, Fenway Park, Boston, Massachusetts, U.S.A.," I told the telegraph clerk. I handed him my form.

The clerk read it through. I pushed Joey's nickel over the counter.

"Trust me," I told Joey as we walked to the door.

On our way out, we heard the clerk beginning to telegraph my message to Larry Doyle. *Tap-tappity-tap-tap. Tappity-tappity-tip.* Just like the beating of a tiny little drum.

8

I Have My Doubts

"I trusted you," Joey said.

We were in our field behind Gilhooley's Brewery. The sun was shining bright. The sky was blue. The grass was green. The smell from the glue factory was blowing the other way. Take it all together, it was a beautiful Fourth of July.

But there was no Larry Doyle to be seen.

Nat, Billy, Seamus, and the rest of the team kept frowning at me during infield practice. I was sitting on Miss Barley's back as she ate grass next to Joey. I looked over Joey's head at the opening in the fence. Any minute now, I was sure Larry Doyle would stick his head through.

Pug's ugly mug showed up instead.

"Here they come," Joey muttered.

The Copperheads all came slithering through the fence, over the fence, around the fence. There were more than I remembered, and they looked ready to skin us alive. They had broomstick bats and old beat-up gloves, just like we did.

"You're batting first," Pug announced.

"Visitors usually bat first," Seamus spoke up.

A kid even bigger than Pug took a practice swing with his bat. It whistled through the air beside Seamus. If Seamus hadn't ducked, he would have been clobbered.

"You're batting first," the kid repeated.

I slid off Miss Barley's back and picked up my broomstick bat.

"Come on," I said to my friends. "Let's play ball."

Our dugout was a bench made of boards

laid across two beer barrels. My team followed me like prisoners going to hard labor.

"Don't worry, fellas," I said. "Larry will come through for us."

"Patrick, you have really done it this time," Billy Pogue said. He sighed.

I called out to Pug on the pitcher's mound. "Are we agreed on the terms?" I asked. "Doyle. Over the fence. Game's over."

The Copperheads were slapping their gloves with their fists, squinting in the sun and looking tough.

Pug threw a change-up to their catcher and then looked my way.

"Got it. Doyle. Over the fence. Game's over. Got that straight, Copperheads?"

He looked around at his gang, and they all howled with laughter.

"So long as you agree," I said, and turned back to our bench.

The fellows on my team were working out the batting order. Each and every one of them wore a graveyard face. Take them all together, they were a gloomy bunch.

"Let's just try to stay in the game," Nat was saying. "As long as we're in it, there's still a chance for Patrick to hit a home run."

This was the moment when I was supposed to remind them about Laughing Larry Doyle. In fact, they all looked at me silently. They were waiting for me to say *I* didn't have to hit a home run.

But my faith was beginning to fade. Just a little bit. Just a little tiny bit. Maybe, just maybe, Larry wasn't going to show up. Maybe it really was up to *Patrick* Doyle.

More than anything else, I wanted to beat those snakes out of our green field. I just didn't think I had the bat to beat them with.

And that was when an angel appeared.

Doyle at the Plate

The kids on my bench had their backs to the fence. They were all facing my way, and I must have taken on a pretty odd look. They stared at me with puzzle written all over their faces.

"He—he—" I stammered, pointing to the entrance.

Larry Doyle, the one-hundred-percent honest and true real captain of the New York Giants, was standing on our field. A real major league baseball bat rested across his shoulder. For the first time in my whole life, I couldn't think of a thing to say.

Joey turned around on the bench, saw who it was, and fell over backwards onto the grass.

"Hello, fellows. Which one of you is Patrick?" Larry asked.

One by one, the Copperheads noticed there was a grownup on the field. Pug stood with his mouth hanging open. He missed the throw from his first baseman.

The ball went sailing past him toward Larry Doyle. Larry caught it over his head, barehanded. Beautiful.

"I'm Patrick!" I finally said. My heart was singing like a harp. I ran to Larry and pumped his hand up and down like a grown man. "Am *I* glad to see you!"

In a moment, we were surrounded by the fellows on my team. They were cheering and shouting and talking about how they knew he would come. They just knew it all along!

"I meant to write to you, Patrick," Larry said to me. "But you never put in your address.

I hope you weren't worried about me showing up."

I shook my head. "Not on your life, Mr. Doyle."

Suddenly, Pug let out a shout. "Hey! I know who that is now! It's Larry Doyle, the slugger! It's a trick! Foul! Foul!"

The Copperheads came boiling over the field like an army of snakes, hissing and crying foul. "You set us up, Doyle!" Pug yelled.

"So what if I did?" I held my ground. "Nobody said you couldn't get your own ringer."

Larry Doyle was listening closely to this argument. He was also taking a good look at Pug and his gang of Copperheads.

Larry took me by the elbow and led me away from the crowd for a private chat. I winked at Joey as we went by. A private chat with Larry Doyle!

When we got to our bench, he took a seat and patted the plank. I sat too.

"I can see this won't work," he said. "I'd like to help you out, Patrick, I really would. But anyone can see, if I go to bat for you, that wouldn't keep those snakes out. They figure they've been tricked. All bets are off, and they'll take over your field anyway."

That old knuckleball was in my throat again. It's a hard thing to swallow when your dreams come true, only they don't work out like you planned.

"What'll we do?" I asked.

Larry's eyebrows went together while he concentrated. He was looking at the ground. He was looking at my bat. My face got hot.

"Is that what you're hitting with?" he asked.

I didn't even have to answer. He could see how I felt.

"Tell you what," Larry said, dropping his voice a little. He looked over his shoulder. Everyone was watching us. "Think you can swing a real bat? You'd have to choke up on it pretty far. But a good bat makes all the difference."

My heart was singing again. "Sure I can, Mr. Doyle. I swung one once before. I'm sure I can do it."

"Then step up to the plate, Patrick. And may the saints keep your eye on the ball."

Independence Day

The Copperheads took the field. Pug gave me one last mean and angry look, and then stalked to the pitcher's mound.

I spit on my hands and rubbed them together. Then I picked up Larry Doyle's baseball bat. The grip was worn smooth as an apple. The pale wood gleamed white in the bright sunlight. It was heavy. Take it all together, it was a fine piece of equipment. I just hoped I could swing it.

"Come on, Patrick," Joey said quietly. "You can do it."

"You can do it," the rest of my friends chimed in.

I glanced over at Larry. He gave me the
thumbs-up sign and nodded. Then I stepped
up to the plate.

The field was very quiet. Beyond the out-
fielders, the fence on the other side of the
paddock where Miss Barley was grazing
looked miles away.

My heart began drumming loud enough for me to hear it inside my head. I choked up on the bat and drew it back.

"Bless me, St. Patrick," I whispered.

And Pug pitched the first ball.

It whistled past me just as I swung as hard as I could. The bat spun me around and pulled me off balance. I staggered a few steps.

"SSSSTRIKE!" the Copperhead catcher hissed.

"Batter batter batter batter!" my pals chanted.

The drumbeats were still pounding in my ears as I squared off over home plate again. Pug wound up and fired another one past me. I staggered off balance again.

"SSSTEEE-RIKE TWO!" the catcher yelled.

I stepped up to the plate again, and I felt someone take hold of the bat. Larry was behind me. He made a sign with his hands that I should choke up a little bit more on the bat. I did, and he nodded and stepped aside.

"Come on, quit coaching!" Pug snarled.

I narrowed my eyes at Pug. I took a deep breath as he wound up. The drumming was louder and louder in my ears. I could also hear Granny McGaffigan's poem.

> Success to bold St. Patrick's fist.
> He was a saint so clever.
> He gave the sneaking snakes a twist
> And banished them forever.

And the next thing I heard was the crack of the bat hitting the ball, and I went stumbling and twisting around again. And everyone looked up into the air with their mouths hanging open. And everyone turned like mechanical figures to watch the ball go flying over Miss Barley's back, over the fence, and disappear into eternity.

"It's Independence Day!" Joey cheered.

"You Copperheads are gone for*ever*!"

All my pals jumped off the bench. They crowded around me and Larry, yelling and slapping me on the back. Beyond them, I saw

the Copperheads slinking away. And they never returned.

That was the year St. Patrick's Day came on the Fourth of July.

A Little Bit of History

Patrick Doyle is a typical kid of 1915. Although he was born in New York City, his parents and grandparents came to the United States from elsewhere—in his case, Ireland. The Doyles and the McGaffigans and thousands of other Irish families had moved to America to make a better life for themselves. The reasons for their move can be summed up in one word: potatoes.

Back in the 1840s, the people of Ireland ate one important food at almost every meal. They ate potatoes for breakfast, lunch, and dinner. Then a terrible potato disease, a blight, hit the country. All the crops failed.

The potatoes turned to black mushy pulp and made people sick. For several years in the late 1840s and 1850s, potatoes rotted in the field. The result of this was that most people in Ireland had nothing to eat. Thousands died of starvation, and many others died when diseases broke out. This disastrous period of Irish history is called the "Great Hunger."

The Great Hunger started poor Irish people moving to America. For the rest of the century, the Irish moved by the thousands to

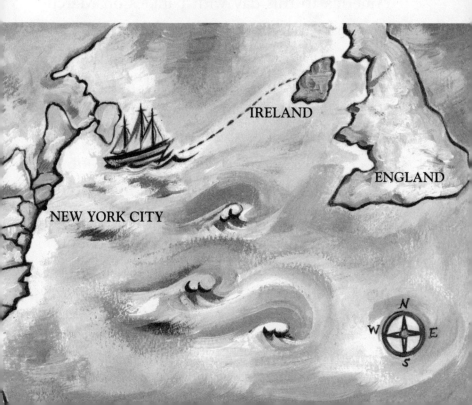

the United States. Many of them settled in the port cities of Boston, New York, and Philadelphia. By the beginning of the 1900s, there were whole neighborhoods that were completely Irish. In fact, the Irish were one of the largest immigrant groups in the United States. They dominated many professions, not just baseball.

The Irish kept many of their traditions, including the celebration of St. Patrick's Day. The patron saint of Ireland is honored in America to this day with parades on March 17. And the Irish continue to love potatoes!

In 1915, America was peaceful, but Europe was fighting World War I. A passenger ship called the *Lusitania* was torpedoed and sunk on its way to the United States, which shocked many Americans. This was one of the events that brought the United States into the terrible war that lasted until 1918.

But at the time of this story, the country and New York City were busy and bustling

and wild about baseball. Some of the greatest heroes of the sport were playing at that time. New York City had three big-league teams: the Giants, the Dodgers, and the Yankees. Larry Doyle played in the National League for a total of fourteen years, and made the World Series three times. In 1915, he led the league with a batting average of .320.

Home runs were a rare thing back then, because the baseballs were much softer than they are today. The old-fashioned baseball didn't have much snap to it, so it didn't go very far. It wasn't until 1919 that the leagues began using a new, fast "jackrabbit," or "home run," ball. Then those jackrabbit balls began jumping out of ballparks all over the country.

Patrick and his friends are like any other baseball fans. Their heroes are giants in their eyes. And Patrick's hero is a New York Giant.

Glossary

arm garters Bands worn around shirtsleeves to keep them neat.

batting stance How a baseball player stands when batting.

brewery A place where beer is made, or brewed.

Charlie Chaplin The most popular movie star of the time, an actor in silent comedies.

El Short for an elevated train, which ran on tracks three stories above the street.

flies-up A batter tosses up a ball and hits it to fielders; a kind of fielding practice.

Hell's Kitchen A poor immigrant neighborhood on the West Side of New York City, with people from many different countries.

67

knuckleball A type of baseball pitch, thrown by gripping the ball with the knuckles or fingertips.

nickelodeon An arcade with game and movie machines that cost a nickel (from *nickel* + *Odeon*, a popular name for theaters or music halls).

pepper A traditional warm-up game for two or more players in which one person throws to a batter, who bunts the ball back.

ringer An expert player used by one team to gain an advantage over the other team.

shamrock A three-leafed clover, one of the symbols of St. Patrick.

shillelagh (shuh-LAY-lee) A short, thick Irish club or stick.

shutout A game in which one side doesn't score any points at all.

spittoon A pot for spitting the juice from chewing tobacco into. Spittoons went out of use when it was discovered that tuberculosis (a deadly lung disease) was spread this way.

stinger A ball that smacks hard into a player's hand, making it "sting."

'talking blarney' How the Irish described stretching the truth or telling a wild story.

tenement An apartment building, usually in a poor neighborhood.

vaudeville A type of entertainment including song and dance, comedy, and magic that was popular at the time.

Western Union The name of a telegraph company.

About the Author

JENNIFER ARMSTRONG has more than a wee drop of green Irish blood in her. She has been talking blarney since she was very young, and like Patrick, she sometimes talked herself into trouble. "I thought it was more fun to make up an exciting story than just tell the humdrum facts. That's really why I became an author."

She has been an author of children's books for many years. Armstrong has written several picture books, as well as historical novels for children. Her first historical novel, *Steal Away*, won the Golden Kite Honor Award from the Society of Children's Book Writers and Illustrators. She lives in Saratoga Springs, New York, and plays Irish songs on the piano.